# STAR WARS™

FEATURES
**STAR WARS**
THE
**MANDALORIAN**
CHARACTERS
& VEHICLES

# OFFICIAL ANNUAL 2023

A bounty hunter's life is full of challenges. Here's one for you to try. Help the Mandalorian find his way through this dangerous maze.

**START**

**FINISH**

This is Greef Karga, an agent of the Bounty Hunters' Guild. Find the differences between Greef Karga and his photos – there's one in every image.

I'M NOT SURE IF I LOOK BETTER WITH OR WITHOUT MY MOUSTACHE.

Look at Mando and Grogu riding their speeder across the desert! Find and tick the piece that is covered by sand.

What does the Mandalorian need on his mission? Find out by colouring each segment in the colour shown by the dot.

The shadows represent heroes and villains. Write the correct letters in the empty boxes to match the characters to their shadows. One has been done for you.

A

A

B

F

D

E

C

Mando has arrived at the Tusken village. Look closely at the two pictures and see if you can spot the ten differences between them.

Watch out, an Imperial Light Cruiser has just landed! Tick all the parts that belong to the cruiser. One has been done for you.

Klatooinian raiders are after Mando in their AT-ST walker. Follow the arrows to find the way they need to go to reach the bounty hunter, and colour in the route.

START

FINISH

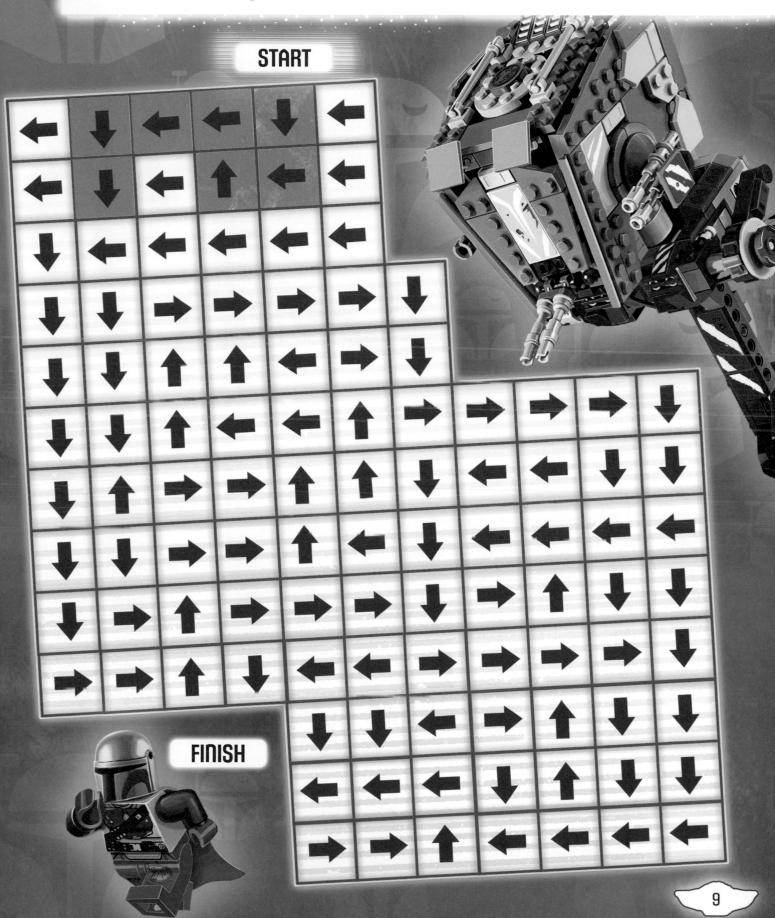

9

Every inhabitant of the galaxy far, far away is unique in their own way. Read the descriptions and write the correct numbers next to the characters.

**1**

The bearded agent of the Bounty Hunters' Guild.

**2**

A bounty hunter who has a helmet with an antenna.

**3**

A Moff who prefers the Darksaber to a blaster.

**4**

A bounty hunter who is a droid.

**5**

A bounty hunter in a long cape.

It looks like all the local Tusken Raiders have gathered here. Find the group shown in the top white box in each of the rows of characters below it.

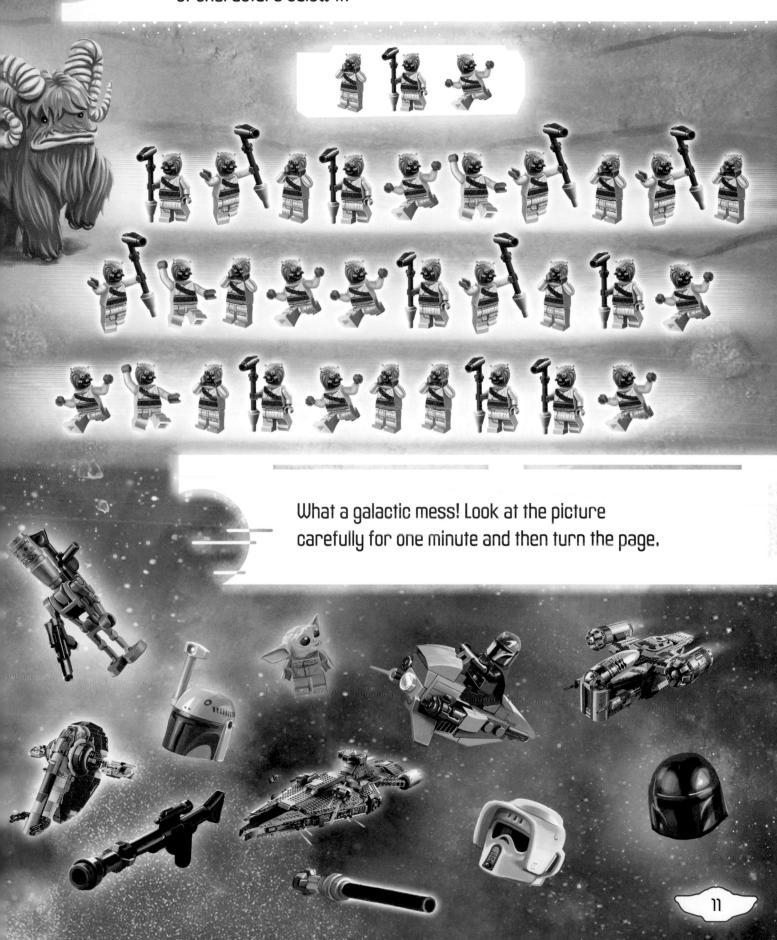

What a galactic mess! Look at the picture carefully for one minute and then turn the page.

After the galactic mess, it's time for a galactic cleanup! Tick all items you remember from the previous page. One has been done for you.

In the last battle, the Imperial Armoured Marauder lost some of its parts. Find out what the vehicle looked like before by drawing in the missing parts to finish the picture.

PHEW! IT'S SUPPOSED TO BE ARMOUR, BUT IT FALLS APART AS EASILY AS A HOUSE OF CARDS.

Oh, no! An Imperial Scout Trooper has attacked the *Razor Crest*'s crew! Look at the boxes under each picture and circle the characters that are not taking part in the fight.

# THE HERO

IT WAS JUST ANOTHER DAY ON PLANET NEVARRO. GREEF KARGA, WHILE WAITING FOR HIS FRIENDS, WAS ENTERTAINING A GROUP OF KIDS WITH A STORY ABOUT A GREAT HERO ...

HE'S TRULY INCREDIBLE! THE GREATEST BOUNTY HUNTERS AND IMPERIAL THUGS ARE AFTER HIM, BUT HE ALWAYS ESCAPES THEIR TRAPS ...

HE'S NOT AFRAID OF GIANT BEASTS. HE CAN LIFT THEM UP INTO THE AIR WITHOUT EVEN TOUCHING THEM!

Finding someone in this galactic crowd is not an easy task! Take on the challenge by matching the identical characters in the groups that are next to each other. The first character has been found for you.

Looking for spare parts for your starship? The Jawas might be able to help. Find all the items from the box in the pile of spare parts.

Fennec Shand isn't afraid of the most powerful opponents!
Circle the mirror image of the brave mercenary.

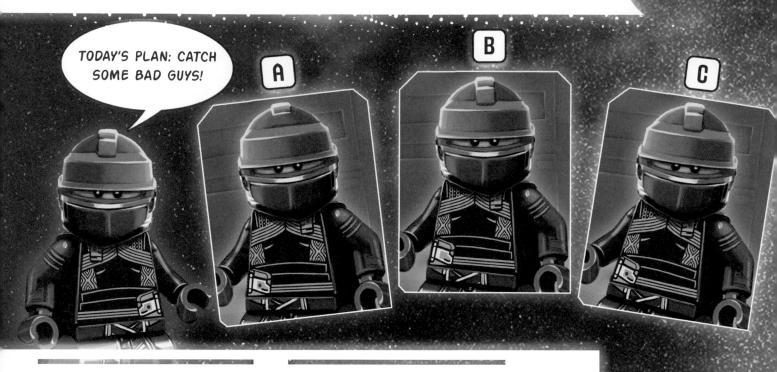

Time to inspect the Mandalorian inventory. Work out
the order in which the helmets are arranged. Write the
numbers of the missing helmets in the blank spaces.

20

Out of the way! The AT-ST is going into action. Take a good look at how this dangerous machine is built and draw lines to put the parts in the correct places.

There's a track full of obstacles ahead of IG-11. Guide the droid so that he passes through and defeats each of the stormtroopers on his way, without using the same path more than once.

Who has the sharpest eye in the galaxy?
Use the clues to find out the answer.

The character you're looking for:
• is armed
• is not a droid
• has dark eyes
• isn't showing his fangs

Untangle the lines to find out who will sit behind the controls of each of these vehicles.

1

2

3

4

After his last mission, Greef Karga isn't looking too good. Help him get back in shape by numbering the picture pieces to put them in the correct order. One has been done for you.

This is the Darksaber. Find the code that is identical to the one below this powerful weapon to discover who has wielded it.

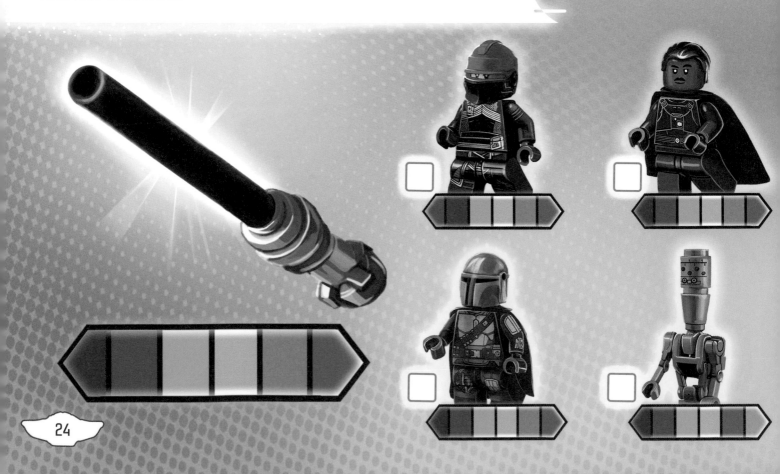

Ready, steady, go! Use the code to colour in the picture and see who is hiding in a galaxy far, far away.

1    2    3    4    5    6    7

One of these vehicles is about to lose power! Which vehicle appears the least number of times? That's the one that needs to start an emergency landing soon!

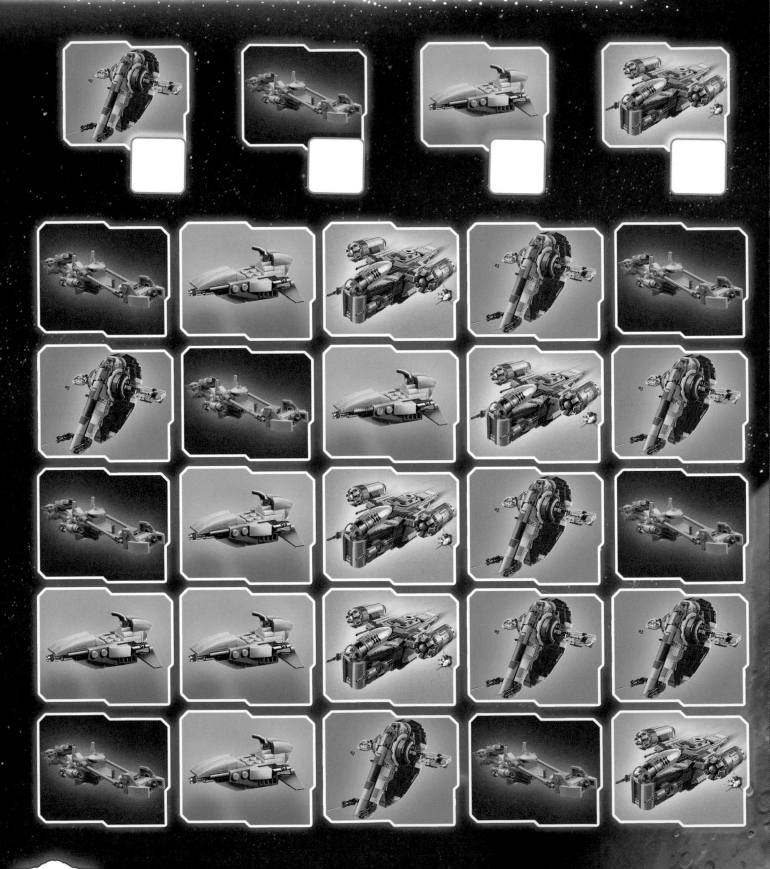

The *Razor Crest* has been spotted! Look at the pictures of starship's parts and check if they are from Mando's starship. Circle 'Y' for 'yes' if they are, and 'N' for 'no' if they aren't.

Y  N

Y  N

Y  N

Y  N

A gang of Klatooinian Raiders is after the Mandalorian! Circle the one thug in each row that's not falling in line with the others. One has been done for you.

Mando belongs to Clan Mudhorn. Discover what the clan's symbol looks like by writing the correct letters in the empty spaces. One has been done for you.

D

E

C

B

A

B

*I MUST ADMIT, THE MUDHORN IS IMPRESSIVE.*

Circle two parts that do not belong to Boba Fett's starship.

There is no time to waste! Find the Mandalorian and Grogu in the picture before the stormtroopers do.

The bounty hunters are joining forces! Draw a path from Boba Fett to the Mandalorian by connecting the same colours in neighbouring fields.

Fall in, Dark Troopers! Circle the three droids that are different to the others.

Boba Fett attacks! Look carefully at the two pictures of the legendary bounty hunter's starship and find eight differences between them.

Oh, no! Not the Klatooinian raiders again . . . Choose the path where Mando will meet the fewest opponents.

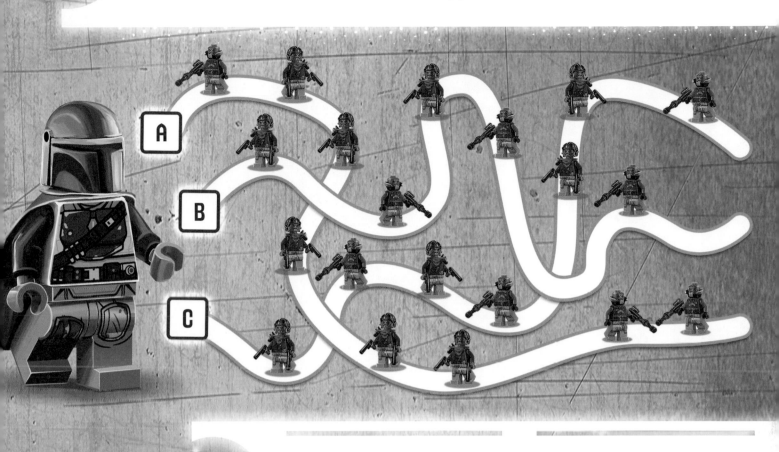

Oops! The carbon-freezing process is out of control. Switch on the defrosting mode and tick the correct defrosted piece missing from the picture.

Take a look at the crowd of Mandalorians from the Nevarro covert and find the groups shown at the bottom of the page. One group has been found for you.

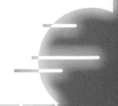

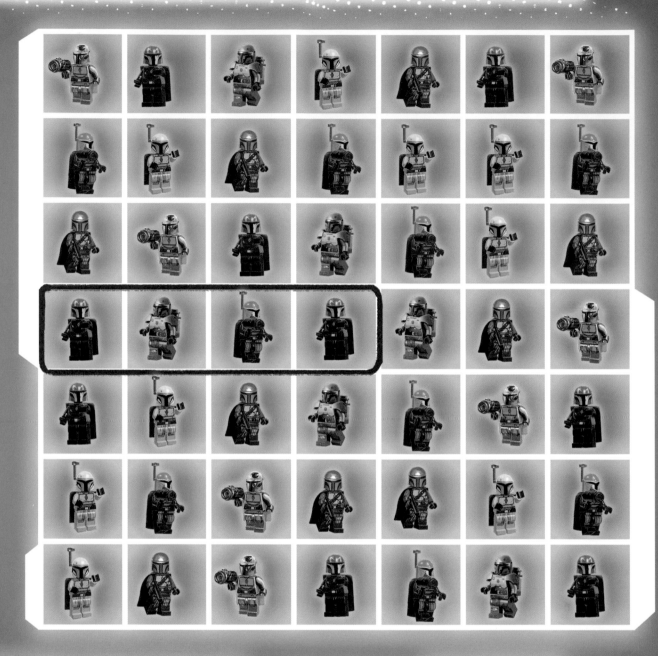

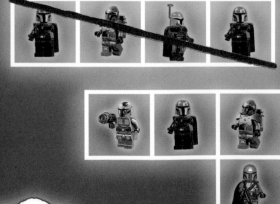

Greef Karga won't forget this encounter in a hurry. Find the drawing that is identical to the scene and colour it in.

A

B

C

An Imperial Light Cruiser is right behind the *Razor Crest*.
Complete the picture by writing the correct numbers in
the empty boxes. One has been done for you.

IG-11 needs a friend to back him up. Help him find Mando among the IG droids.

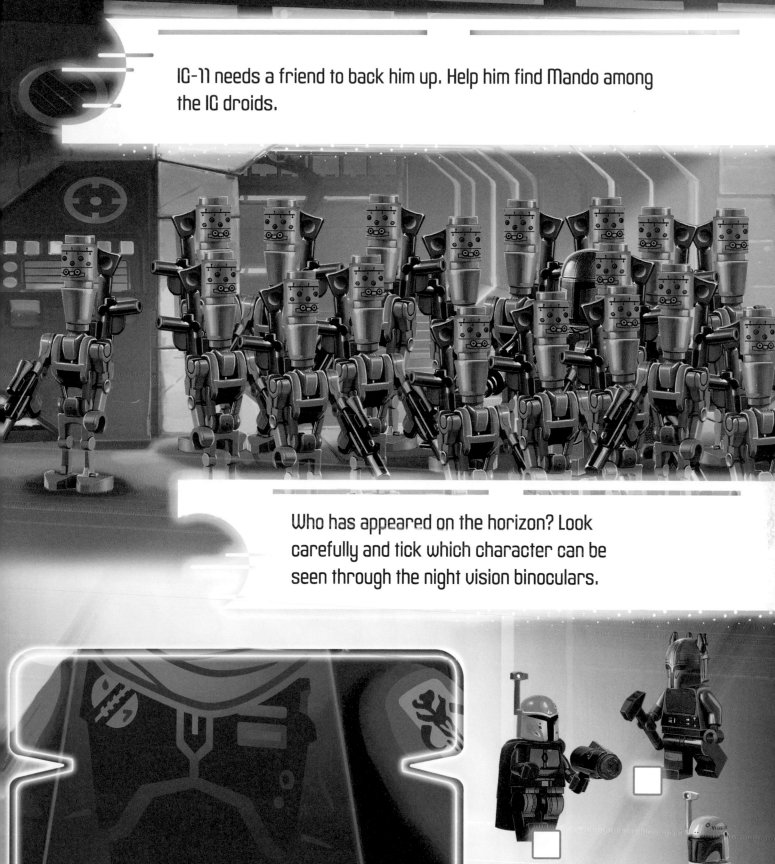

Who has appeared on the horizon? Look carefully and tick which character can be seen through the night vision binoculars.

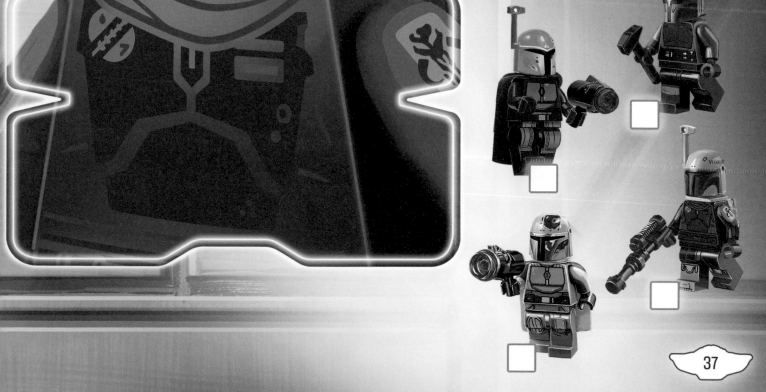

Help Boba Fett's starship navigate by colouring the way
out of this galactic tangle, going over and under other paths.

Attention! Static transmission! Figure out who the blurry portraits are and write the correct letters in the empty boxes.

A

B

C

D

# DON'T MESS WITH THE KID!

SOMEWHERE IN A GALAXY FAR, FAR AWAY, OLD FRIENDS ARE SITTING IN A BAR DISCUSSING BUSINESS ...

I HAVE A JOB FOR YOU ON TATOOINE, MANDO.

HOW MUCH WILL I GET FOR IT?

ENOUGH TO BUY NEW ARMOUR FOR YOU AND MILK FOR THE KID.

HEY, KARGA! WHY DOES HE KEEP GETTING ALL THE BEST JOBS?

YOU'RE NEGLECTING US! WE'RE LOSING EARNINGS BECAUSE OF HIM!

WELL, I HAVE TOUGH JOBS AND YOU GUYS JUST AREN'T IN HIS LEAGUE.

WHAAAAT?! US NOT IN HIS LEAGUE?! I'LL SHOW YOU!

THIS KID IS PRECIOUS! AN IMPERIAL BIGWIG IS LOOKING FOR HIM! LET'S TAKE HIM! IT WILL MAKE UP FOR ALL OUR LOSSES!

The Mandalorian armour is made of super-durable beskar steel. Find ten bars of this valuable metal in the Armourer's Forge. One has been found for you.

I TOOK A MILLION DIRECT BLASTER SHOTS AND MY ARMOUR STILL LOOKS GOOD AS NEW!

Has anyone seen another lightsaber? Match the identical weapons into pairs by colouring in the circles next to them with the same colours.

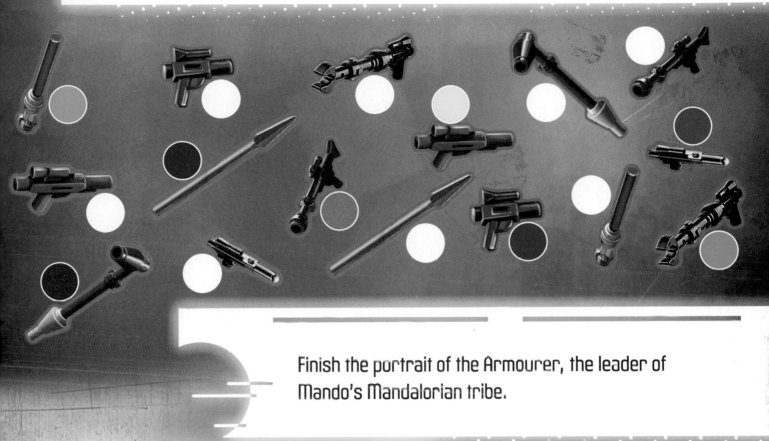

Finish the portrait of the Armourer, the leader of Mando's Mandalorian tribe.

SILVER HELMETS ARE MUCH MORE TRENDY IF YOU ASK ME.

The Holocron has been unlocked! Find out who will appear in it and number the pictures from the most to the least blurred. One has been done for you.

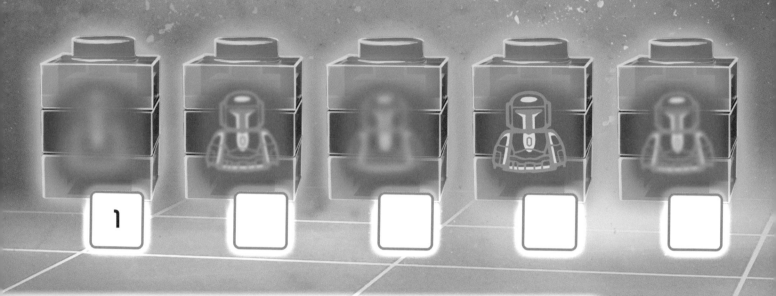

1

Quick! Before he heads out of sight, tick the shadow that belongs to the Mandalorian warrior riding his speeder across the desert.

Grogu doesn't like staying still. Which circle contains four different poses of the Child?

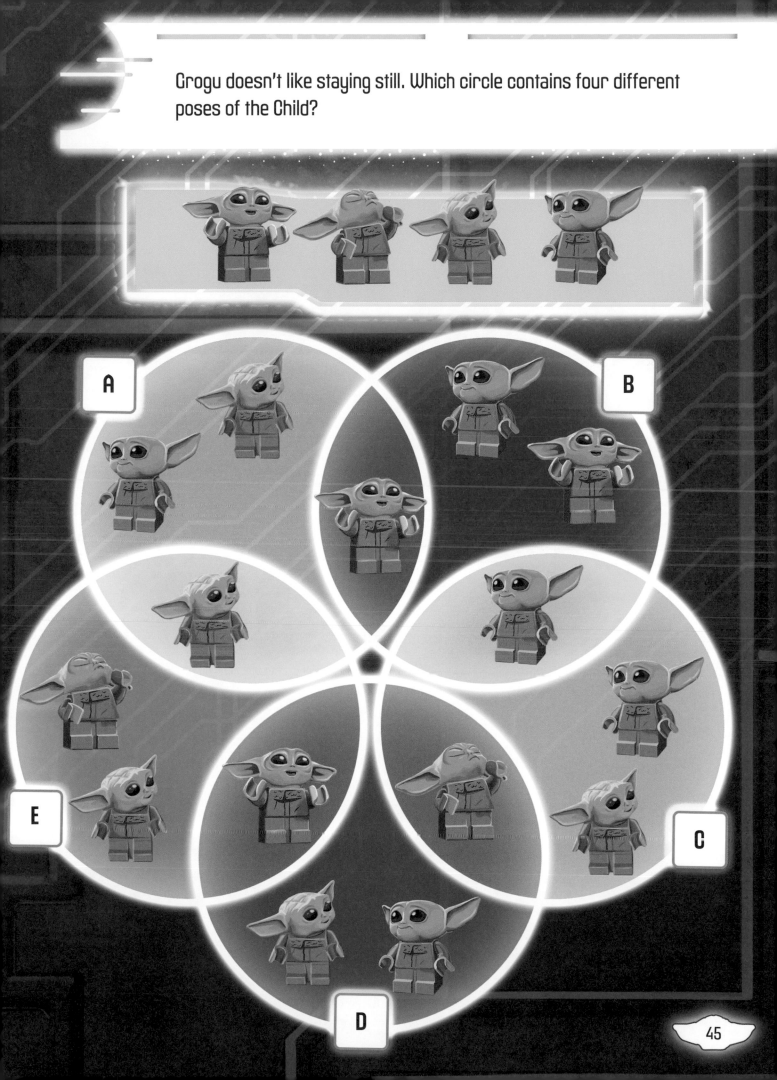

Bounty hunter Fennec Shand is in trouble. But who will rescue her? Look for the character whose pictures are all different.

I HATE BEING IN TROUBLE.

Excellent sharpshooter skills! Tick the white box next to the target that Greef Karga has hit the most times.

Which stormtrooper will stand in IG-11's way? Untangle the jagged paths to find out.

A

B

C

Boba Fett's starship is bent out of shape after another galactic
battle. Fix it by connecting each set of coloured dots in turn.

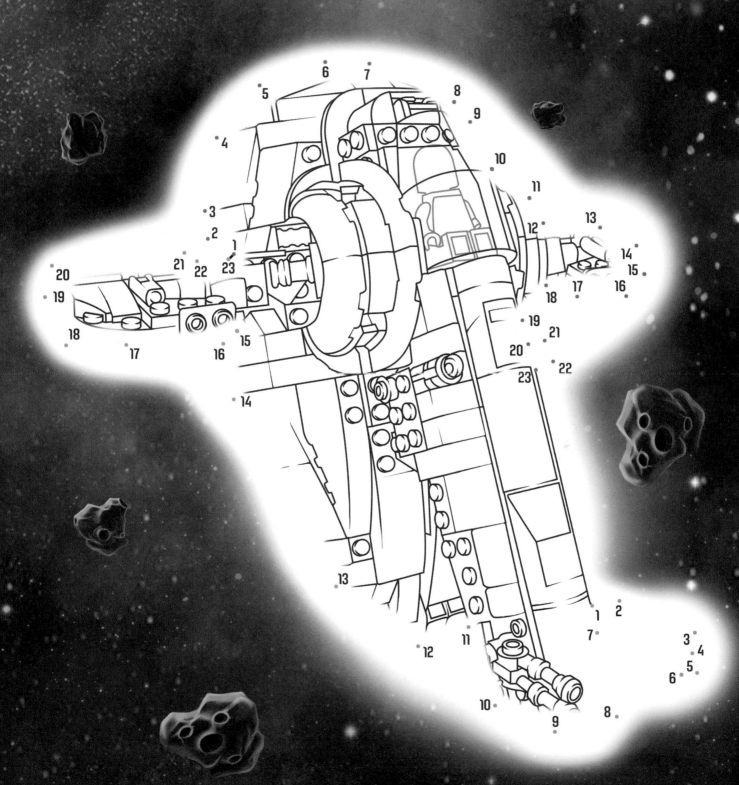

Way to go! Mando has finally joined his fellow Mandalorians. Find and circle the two teams of warriors in the shapes at the top in the rows below them.

In the heat of the action, everything got mixed up! Sort out the pieces of the picture by numbering them to put them in the correct order. One has been done for you.

1  2  3  4  5                    1

Breathing masks are a trademark of the Sand People. Follow the steps to draw a Tusken Raider's mask.

The long sticks used by the Tusken Raiders are called *gaderffii*. Number the Tusken weapons in the order they need to be picked up from the stack. The top one has been picked up for you.

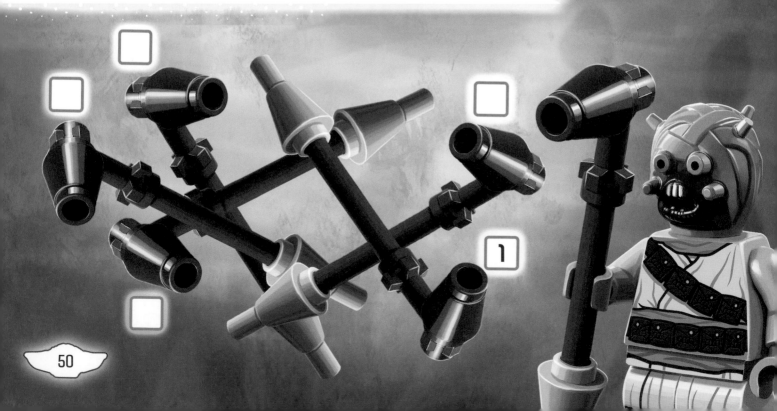

The galactic warriors rarely part with their weapons. Work out which warrior's weapon is missing from each of the circles and write its number in the blank space. One has been done for you.

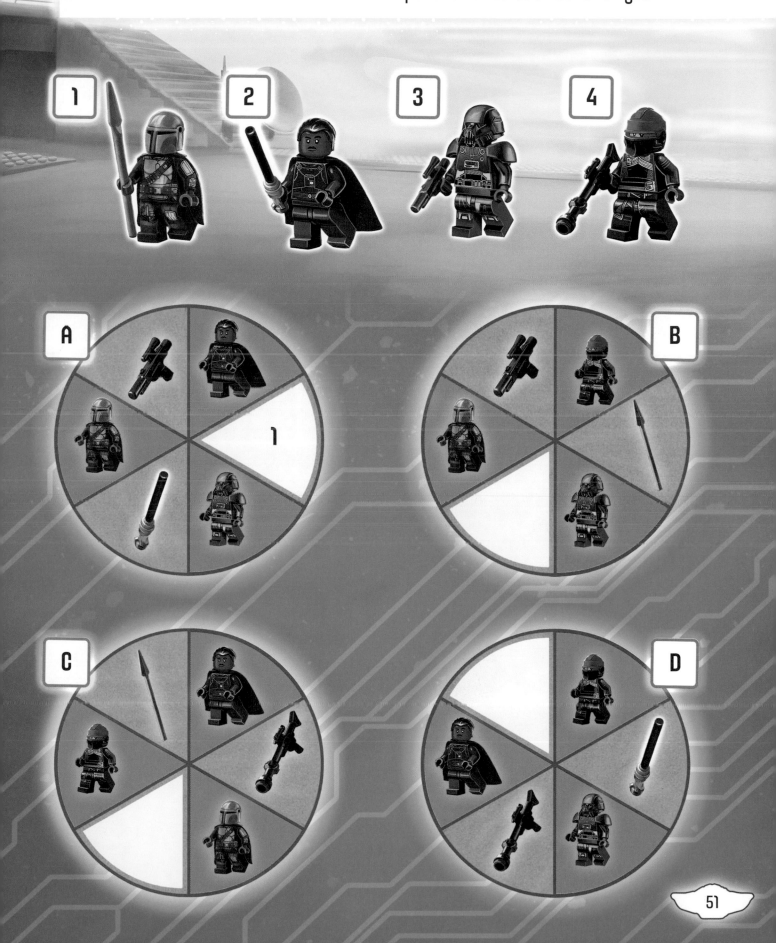

Attention! An Imperial Light Cruiser has appeared on the radar! Find its weak points and mark them with correct colours on the screen. One has been found for you.

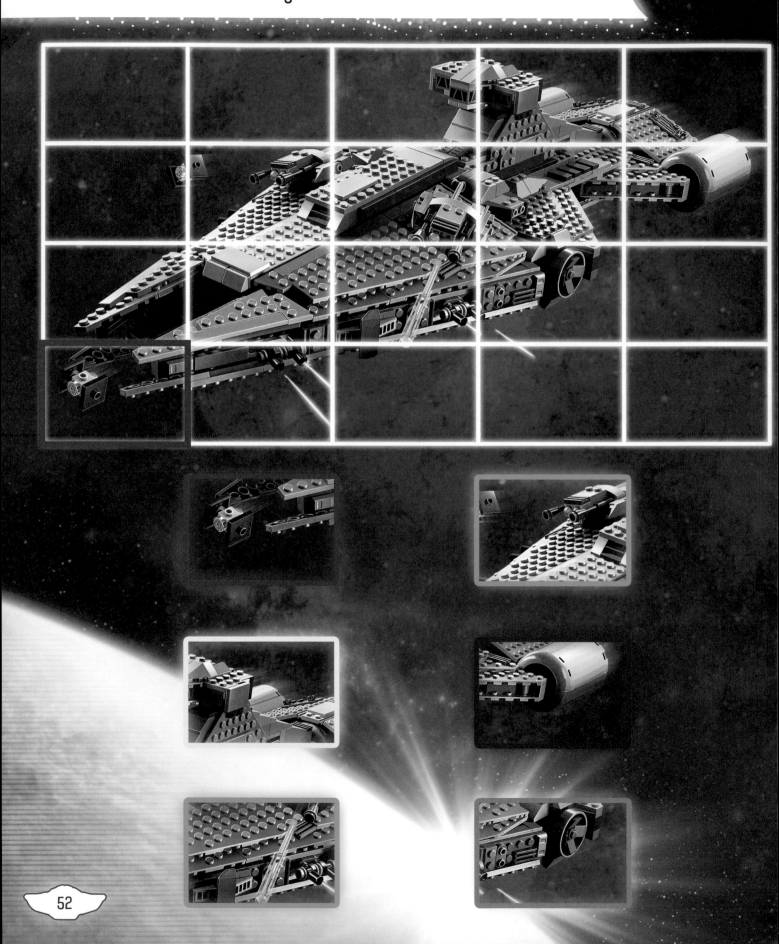

Greef Karga isn't afraid to face a heavily-armed foe like the artillery stormtrooper. Use the colour code to guide Greef to his opponent.

# MASTER BUILDER

AFTER A LONG AND BUMPY JOURNEY (AND A DANGEROUS ONE, TOO), THE BATTERED RAZOR CREST ARRIVES ON TATOOINE ...

HOLD ON TO SOMETHING, KID! WE'LL BE LUCKY IF WE LAND IN ONE PIECE!

SHE'S IN WORSE SHAPE THAN I THOUGHT!

I'M GOING SHOPPING FOR SPARE PARTS. I'LL BE BACK SOON.

UM?

NO! YOU STAY INSIDE UNTIL I RETURN, KID! GOT IT?

??? ...

SOME TIME LATER ...

HEY! DIDN'T I TELL YOU TO ...

WOW! I DIDN'T KNOW YOU WERE SUCH A MASTER BUILDER!

SOOO ... PERHAPS YOU COULD USE YOUR BUILDING SKILLS TO HELP ME FIX THE SHIP NOW?

This ballista could use some fixing. Put the shooting device together by writing the letters of the missing parts in the white shapes. One has been done for you.

Now that the ballista is ready to use, choose someone to operate it. Follow the colour code from portrait to portrait and you'll find the best candidate.

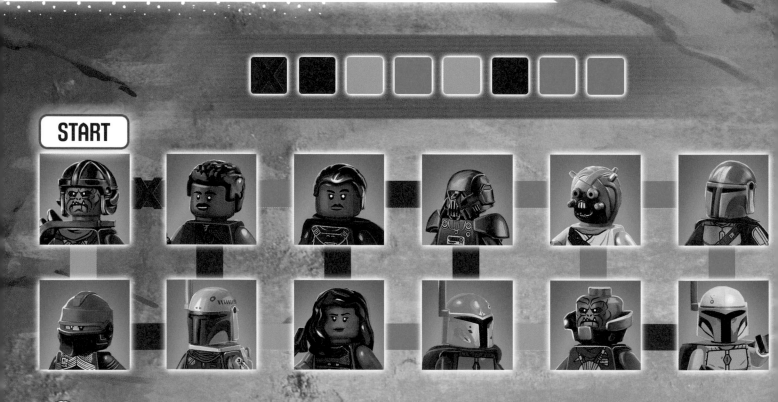

START

It's time for Mando to part with Grogu. Draw lines to connect the identical symbols. The character that is not crossed by any line will take care of the Child from now on. One line has been drawn for you.

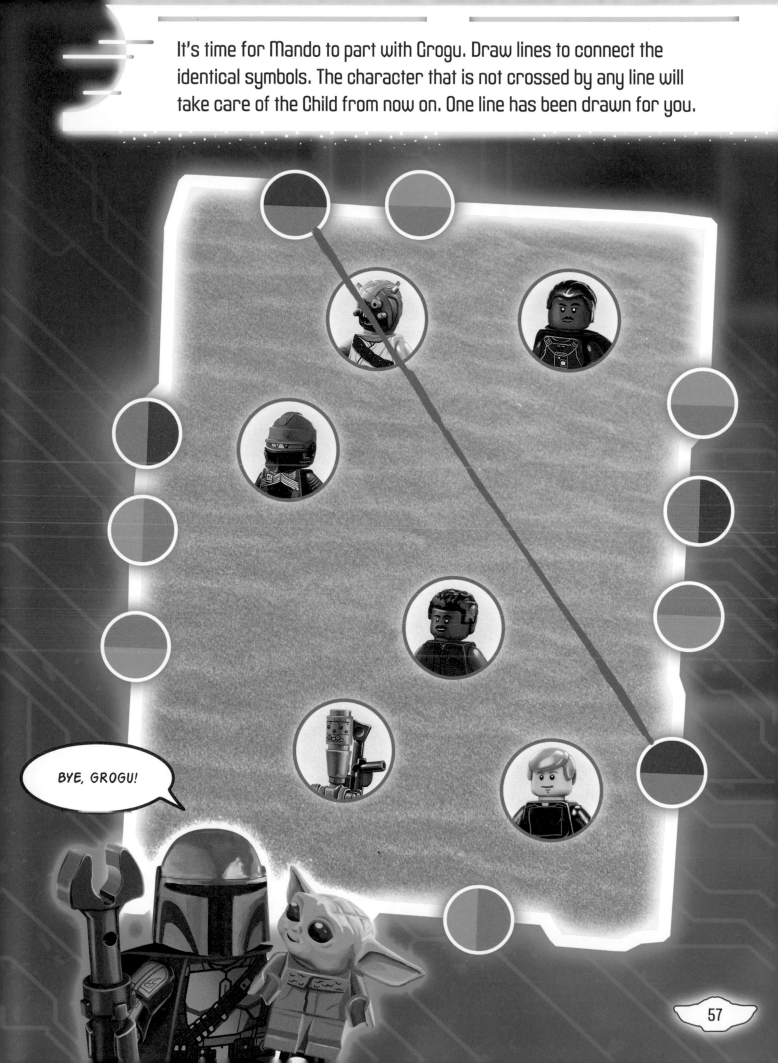

BYE, GROGU!

# ANSWERS

p. 4

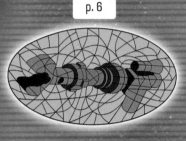

p. 5

p. 5

p. 6

p. 6

p. 7

p. 8

p. 9

p. 10

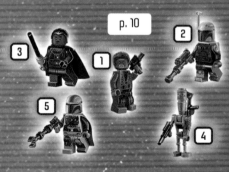

p. 11

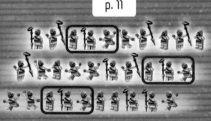

p. 12

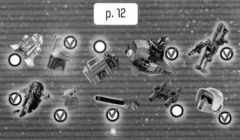

p. 13

p. 18

p. 19

p. 20

C

p. 20

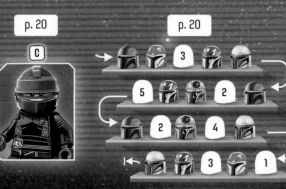

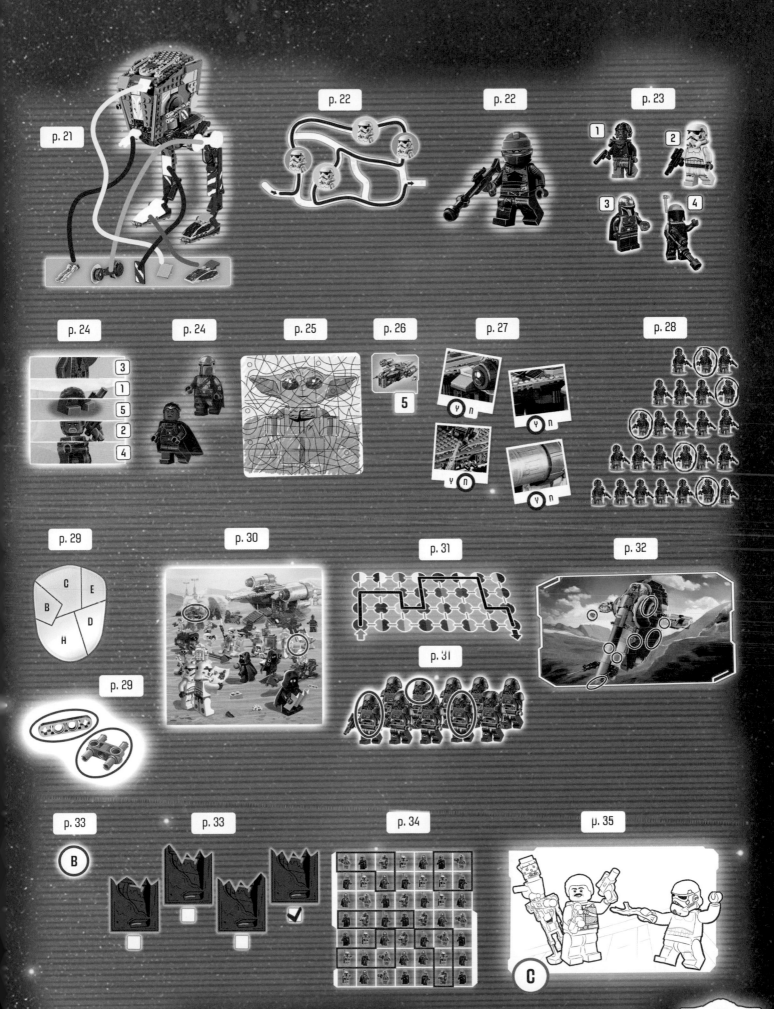

p. 21

p. 22

p. 22

p. 23

1
2
3
4

p. 24

3
1
5
2
4

p. 24

p. 25

p. 26

5

p. 27

Y n
Y n
Y n
Y n

p. 28

p. 29

C
E
B
D
H

p. 29

p. 30

p. 31

p. 31

p. 32

p. 33

B

p. 33

p. 34

μ. 35

C

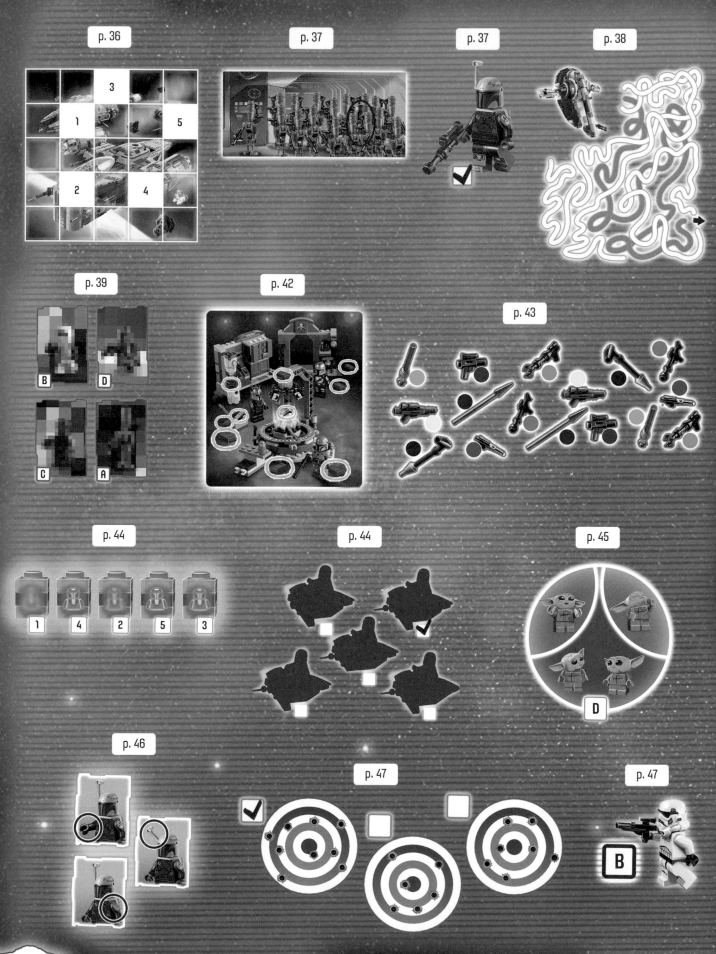

p. 36

p. 37

p. 37

p. 38

p. 39

p. 42

p. 43

p. 44

p. 44

p. 45

D

p. 46

p. 47

p. 47

B

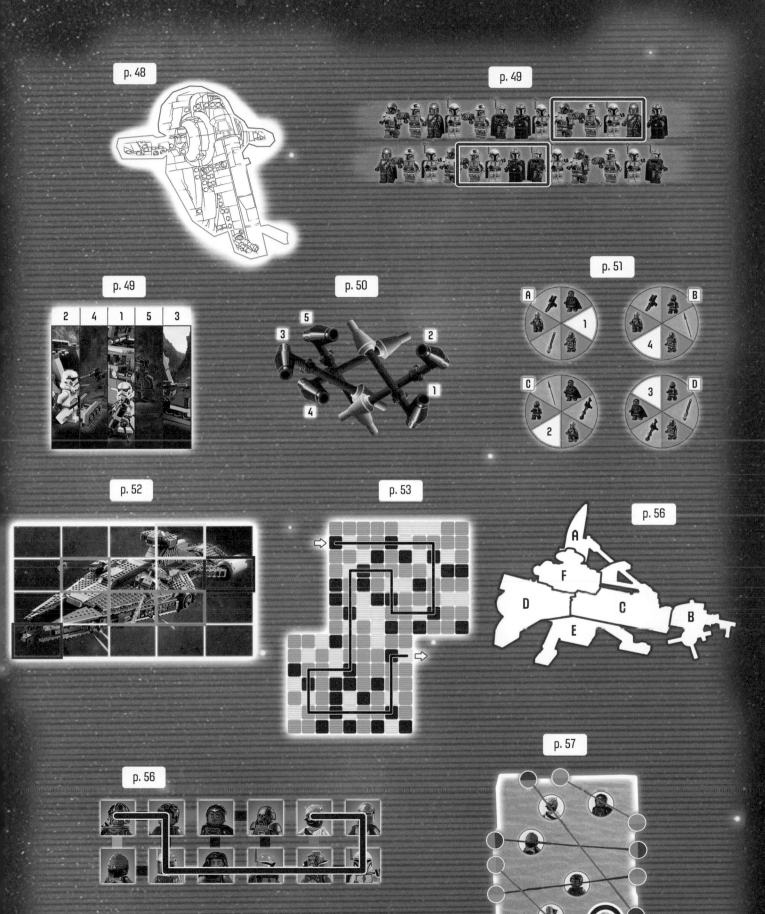

p. 48

p. 49

p. 49

| 2 | 4 | 1 | 5 | 3 |

p. 50

p. 51

A    B

C    D

p. 52

p. 53

p. 56

p. 56

p. 57